DUMB LUCK

DUMB LUCK

Poems by
SAM HAMILL

BOA Editions, Ltd. ✦ Rochester, NY ✦ 2002

First Edition
02 03 04 05 7 6 5 4 3 2 1

Publications by BOA Editions, Ltd.—
a not-for-profit corporation under section 501 (c) (3)
of the United States Internal Revenue Code—
are made possible with the assistance of grants from
the Literature Program of the New York State Council on the Arts,
the Literature Program of the National Endowment for the Arts,
the Sonia Raiziss Giop Charitable Foundation,
the Lannan Foundation,
as well as from the Mary S. Mulligan Charitable Trust,
the County of Monroe, NY, Citibank,
Ames-Amzalak Memorial Trust,
and The CIRE Foundation.

See page 104 for special individual acknowledgments.

Cover Design: Lisa Mauro / Mauro Design
Cover Painting: "Egret and Grapes" by David Kroll, courtesy of the artist and the
    Grover / Thurston Gallery
Interior Design and Typesetting: Richard Foerster
Manufacturing: McNaughton & Gunn, Lithographers
BOA Logo: Mirko

LIBRARY OF CONGRESS CATALOGING-IN-PUBLICATION DATA

Hamill, Sam.
  Dumb luck : poems / by Sam Hamill.
    p. cm. — (American poets continuum series ; no. 75)
  ISBN 1-929918-25-9
  I. Title. II. Series.

PS3558.A4235 D86 2002
811'.54—dc21

                                                        2002074576

BOA Editions, Ltd.
Steven Huff, Publisher
H. Allen Spencer, Chair
A. Poulin, Jr., President & Founder (1938–1996)
260 East Avenue, Rochester, NY 14604
www.boaeditions.org

For Peter Lewis
for Eron Hamill and Gray Foster
for Hayden and Joe-Anne
and for Steve and Thom and Sarah

"I have had to learn the simplest things
last. Which made for difficulty."
                    —Charles Olson

*

Yun-men was asked, "What are a whole lifetime's
teachings?"

"A clear statement."

Contents

Part One

In Memoriam, Morris Graves

Rising from my *zafu* just as dawn breaks
over the trees, below a few thin clouds
that will burn off in an hour, I'm pleased
cherry and plum trees bloom, daffodil flowers
falling or fallen, and the garden glows
in various shades of yellow and green.
This house I built so long ago grows old.
The garden and the life are a poem
evolving from traditions old as time.
I came here green, unwise. I'm still unwise.
Like the old Buddhist poets who taught me
how to live, I believe the poem is
a sacramental act, pure devotion
to whatever may be revealed only
through the music of intuition. The
dance of the intellect, the dance of wild
imagination, illuminates what
cannot otherwise be known—a kōan,
one's rational and irrational mind
at one. It is so because leaves are green,
and death is born in greenness; and it's true
as blue and right as rain, and sustains me
in my practice. As Carolyn Kizer
remarked on Chinese poetry, wisely,
"It teaches us the value of friendship.
And you may not believe it, but that's far
more important than husbands, wives, even
children. Because what are you if you are
not first of all a friend?"
                               So now I turn
in my fifty-eighth year to face Tu Fu,
who died, in exile, at my age. And, "I
have beaten out my exile," Ezra wrote

in a hard time years before Rapallo.
My exile is not alienation,
but rootedness, poetry's sustenance.
My daily friends are robins listening
for worms, busy finches, jays, noisy crows,
a woodpecker now and then. And Morris,
who painted the wind. "The painting has no
narrative. It is exactly what it is,
flowers and light." And the poem has no
paraphrase, but embodies what it is—
found only in its singing. The *cante
jondo*, "to keep bitterness from sorrow."
I will not mourn the death of one so true.
I raise my cup and bow and make this song
because a few friends have sustained me,
and embody what poetry has taught me.

Chuang Tzu and the First Noble Truth

As Chuang Tzu would say
when some good Confucian talked
about righteousness
and virtue, "Not quite there yet,
eh?" knowing that words can say

only so much, that
behind the words are more words,
and more behind those.
What the old man understood
is that each word names, and by

naming, it divides:
this from that and on and on.
But the Tao is one.
What is good is good for *whom*?
Do dogs have Buddha nature?

Say yes or say no,
and Buddha nature is gone.
The practice refines
itself. All the words I've loved
so many years? Going, gone.

Buddha nature, Tao,
the practice of poetry—
going, going, gone.
Present mind and future mind
lie beyond what is contained.

What mind do we bring
to the poem or to bed?
Stuck in samsara,

dreaming of truth and virtue,
just who is that butterfly,

just who is that man
who says again with a grin
and shake of the head,
"Struggle and judgment and pain—
still not quite there yet, eh?"

Essay on Rhyme

"After the final no there comes a yes
on which the future world depends," I think
Stevens wrote. It doesn't matter that I
have failed to look it up as much as that
I remember it after all these years—

I never warmed to Stevens in college
where I first read him. Oh yes, I admired
his technical virtuosity, his
sometimes expansive imagination.
He was a little too French for my taste,

preferring as it were polite culture to
the sometimes rude convictions a poetry
of the heart imposes like a handprint
eternally bloodied by our history.
But why look for any handprint at all?

Why not be satisfied then with what one
comes to—the poem as a kind of Zen
thusness, the kōan or "case" presented,
finally, with eloquent dispassion?
That's great for Stevens. But not for me.

Another Fool

My friend Doug's reading
Zen Flesh Zen Bones, and admits
he doesn't know Zen.
"If Zen has no gates," he asks,
"just how, then, does one pass through?"

I tell him, "That's right!"
In Thailand, they are appalled
seeing fat Buddhas
brought from China or Japan.
Their Buddha was always lean.

I'm no one's teacher
and never have been. Among
the ten thousand paths
to the Buddha, I follow
only one. The flowering

dharma seeks its own
truest nature, sending roots
deep into cultures
unknown only mere moments
before. I sit with ancient

sages, but have learned
very little. The eagle
circling high above
these hills knows much more than I,
his mantra a plaintive cry

to the human ear
that hears without perception.
Listen: what you hear
and what is there are not two.
Your teacher's another fool.

Be still. Be present. Be here.

Weasel, Crow, and Coyote on the Dharma Trail

A weasel went out
one day and saw a large crow
dancing in the dust.
"Ha-ha," the crow cried, "Ha-ha."
Poor Weasel, not speaking Crow,

thought the old crow
was humiliating him.
"I'll get you for that!"
he barked, "I'll gnaw on your bones!"
Weasel crouched low in the grass

and slowly crept close.
But when he made his great leap,
he came up with dust.
"I'll get you for that!" he barked,
retreating into shadows.

Crow bobbed on his bough.
"Ha-ha, ha-ha," he bellowed.
Weasel leaped again,
snapping the air with his jaws,
"You arrogant prick!" he screamed,

"I'll get you for that!"
Far off, another crow called,
"What's all the ruckus?"
Crow chuckled and replied, "Just
stupid Weasel eating dust.

I tried to warn him
about Coyote," Crow called,
"but all he wanted
was to eat me, then got mad
when I escaped. What a fool!"

Weasel slunk away
with his tail between his legs.
Crow called Coyote,
"Hey, old friend, here comes Weasel,
all tired out from meanness.

I tried to warn him,
but he's too mean to listen."
Coyote grinned. He
licked his chops and sniffed the air.
"The angry ones are easiest."

The Anger of Su Tung-p'o

The great Sung Dynasty nature poet Su Tung-p'o was renowned for his genial, sober character, but everyone knew better than to discuss certain court poets in his presence. On the subject of their moral ostentation and spiritual pedantry, he spoke with uncharacteristic virulence.

In 1070, while serving on a commission appointed by Emperor Ying Tsung, Su incurred the wrath Wang An-shih and the literary status quo, and was subsequently demoted to a minor post in Hangchow. Several years later, demoted once again and serving in Hu-chou, he aroused the suspicions of a censor, was imprisoned for three months, then banished to the wilderness villages of Hupeh province.

Following the death of his nemesis, Wang An-shih, in 1086, Su was recalled to the capital. He was banished again in 1094, recalled, and banished again in 1097. In 1100, he was pardoned and appointed to a position in his provincial capital. He died on the 28th day of the 7th moon of 1101.

"I carefully record details for study by future generations," he wrote, "so that events that might otherwise have vanished into the void may be examined." In 1073, he wrote, "That which flowers must decay. Yet the bureaucrats of the State will stop at nothing in their self-serving attempt to postpone the inevitable." Questioned about his lack of tact, he observed, "When I try to bite my tongue I feel as though I've tried to swallow something that refuses to go down. I must spit it out or gag."

A renowned painter and calligrapher, he copied out the collected poems of T'ao Ch'ien and composed poems drawing freely from the poetry of T'ao Ch'ien, Po Chu-i and others. "The great old masters painted the spirit, not the form of things," he said. "Those who transcend mere form to capture true spirit are very rare. Do these principles, which apply so auspiciously to painting, not apply to verse?"

He is credited with a major beautification project at West Lake. He built bridges. He was a Confucian, Taoist, and Buddhist scholar who infuriated Confucian hypocrites. Yet, he is most famous for professing on behalf of simplicity and "primitiveness" as the essence of style, saying he wrote "like water flows—it flows when it should flow and it stops when it should stop."

"Political power," he said, "is, of itself, neither good nor bad, but rises naturally. Like mushrooms growing in manure."

The New York Poem

I sit in the dark, not brooding
exactly, not waiting for the dawn
that is just beginning, at six-twenty-one,
in gray October light behind the trees.
I sit, breathing, mind turning on its wheel.

Hayden writes, "What use is poetry
in times like these?" And I suppose
I understand when he says, "A poet
simply cannot comprehend
any meaning in such slaughter."

Nevertheless, in the grip of horror,
I turn to poetry, not prose,
to help me come to terms—
such as can be—with the lies, murders
and breathtaking hypocrisies

of those who would lead a nation
or a church. "What use is poetry?"
I sat down September twelfth,
two-thousand-one in the Common Era,
and read Rumi and kissed the ground.

And now that millions starve
in the name of holy war? Every war
is holy. It is the same pathetic story
from which we derive
"biblical proportion."

I hear Pilate's footsteps ring
on cobblestone, the voice of Joe McCarthy
cursing in the Senate, Little Boy exploding
as the whole sky shudders.
In New York City, the crashes

and subsequent collapses
created seismic waves. To begin to speak
of the dead, of the dying . . . how
can a poet speak of proportion any more
at all? Yet as the old Greek said,

We walk on the faces of the dead.
The dark fall sky grows blue.
Alone among ash and bones and ruins,
Tu Fu and Basho write the poem.
The last trace of blind rage fades

and a mute sadness settles in,
like dust, for the long, long haul. But if
I do not get up and sing,
if I do not get up and dance again,
the savages will win.

I'll kiss the sword that kills me if I must.

Poem in the Margins of the *Shōyō Roku*

Yun-yan asked Tao-wu,
"What does the Bodhisattva
of Compassion do
with a thousand hands and eyes?"
"She reaches for the pillow."

"Now I understand:
all over our bodies, then,
there are hands and eyes."
"You got eighty percent." "Oh?"
"Throughout the body—eyes, hands."

The awakened mind
reviles the deluded mind
of moments before.
The emperor's clothes reveal
all that a thief has stolen.

Awakening

In early morning
fog, the great cedars emerge,
still wearing bed-clothes

First Snow

The first heavy snow
in the Olympic Mountains
brings them much closer

Zuihitsu

Oinomi wa
hi no nagai ni mo
namida kana
                —Issa

I sat down to write
something like the *zuihitsu,*
the almost formless
form that may be the source of
the Japanese "pillow book,"

which is not—as some
seem to think—about erotic
life exclusively,
except inasmuch as life
itself defines erotic

reality in
the flesh that blossoms within
and grows and withers
in its seemingly endless
return to original source.

The erotic, like
the pillow book, is composed
almost at random,
its inspiration drawn from
all daily experience.

Thus *zuihitsu* has
no predetermined form, no
prescribed subject or
manner, only the almost
random associations

that one thing reveals
about another. So that
when my Japanese
friend remarked of a young girl
that she had *daikon ashi,*

I misunderstood,
thinking that what he meant was
radishes as big
as a girl's leg, where he meant
legs as white as a radish.

In his neighborhood,
all the doors to homes have signs
of one character:
enu, dog. That says it all.
The old woman arriving

for morning sutras
an hour before dawn asked me
whether I'm Buddhist.
I said, "Yes, I'm Zen." She said,
"This isn't a Zen temple."

"That's okay," I said,
"I don't understand the words
anyway." She grinned
almost toothlessly and said,
"Neither do these young monks.

They think they will live
forever." I remember
Birkin's instructions
on the proper way to eat
a fig in *Women in Love.*

It's far more purely
erotic than poor Lady
Chatterly weaving
flowers into her lover's
pubic hair. Sei Shonagon

is far more discreet,
but no less revealing, each
entry in her great
pillow book composed with such
intimacy as can be

illuminating—
not by style or by subject,
but by quality
of attention invested
in each luminous detail.

After months of rain,
a cold clear sky and bright sun
to welcome the Year
of the Rabbit. The plump tongues
of apricot, peach and plum

are waiting to be
tasted in the mouths of those
departed lovers
of a thousand years ago.
Sei Shonagon died in rags,

in utter squalor,
unheralded and unloved,
even her own name
erased from all she'd written.
I'll go out in the garden

when it's warm enough
and sit on a stump or stone
and think of nothing.
Although we have never met,
although we are worlds apart,

you made my heart beat
just a little more clearly
today. What you gave
and all that I took away.
Across culture and gender,

across time and space,
in this old book of the heart,
one small notation
follows the next and the next.
The world of ten thousand things,

and within each, amazing grace.

Fifteen Stitches

Long after midnight,
I lie awake, bedroom lit
by cherry blossoms

★

Dawn, a turquoise sky,
sun glistening on water—
I sigh, When I die . . .

★

With bread and coffee
and a little bow, I greet
the emerging day

★

A robin wades through
deep green grass, its rusty breast
dripping yellow dew

★

Turquoise sky, green grass
first warm summer days—these are
delirious dreams

★

Yesterday a crow
snatched Tom's lunch from his golf cart
while he was putting

★

I want to know what
the crow knows, what the lark sings,
the woodpecker's code

*

I sat and listened
to nothing. And then, somewhere,
an alder leaf fell

*

The coyote paused
ten feet from the porch, sniffed three
times, and trotted off

*

How princely in its
rag-bag patchwork tattered coat,
that old coyote

*

Now summer begins,
the woods, the sky, even dreams—
all tinged yellow green

*

Little lavender
irises burst into bloom—
one, two, eleven

*

The seventieth
day of bombing Kosovo—
mouse turds in the oats

*

Bashō's summer grass
billows in the breezes of
what enlightened mind

*

In the spider's lair,
the struggling mosquito finds
its own true nature

Sisyphus

It's strange, isn't it,
waking up to realize
one day that you've gone
over the hill, as they say,
and are facing the short side

of your string of days—
as Chuang Tzu aptly put it—
and then you begin
to face, not urgency, not
fear of death, but real comfort

in saying, So this
is what I've become, this is
the man I am and
now I can take it easy,
except that there ought to come

a time when the last
trace of last night's moon shining
in the water won't
move us to the edge of tears,
free of Sisyphean tasks,

when a beautiful
woman is not enough to
bring us dutifully
to our knees, or when the need
to undulate with warblers

floating on a breeze
is enough to make you scream.
Sisyphus was young.
He pushed the huge stone of self
until he became undone.

Even the stories
are sweeter for the young—who
drink too deeply
often enough and wander
in a semi-drunken state

of equal parts bliss
and all seven deadly sins.
In a warm spring rain,
the first cherry blossoms fall,
covering the path like snow.

Issa would be pleased.
I wouldn't be young again
for any damned thing.
Here's Mathios Paskalis
still among those Greek roses,

and, Seferis says,
his nose has grown wrinkled while
his pipe keeps smoking
as he descends the stone steps
that never come to an end.

I am beginning
at last to understand what
Seferis really
meant when he said, "I want
no more than to speak simply,

to be granted that
grace." Simplicity's the end,
just a period
at the end of a compound
complex sentence, the great stone

of Sisyphus seen
from the hill's other side.
Let old men converse
across the abyss of time. We'll
watch salamanders couple

in a green pool's shade
and remember the passions
we indulged when we
were forty-five. Old age comes
more quickly than Yangtze floods.

And it's not all bad.
We can set a sturdy pace.
When there's nothing left
to prove, simplicity is
the very nature of things.

Chuang Tzu's fisherman
brought Confucius to his knees.
To follow the way,
he says with his sly grin, is
to finally reach completion.

Which is not an end,
but a means. Sisyphean
tasks, like lost causes,
are the only ones worthwhile.
And then the robin sings.

Part Two

Lives of a Poet: Saigyō's Solitude

In the Rice Fields of Hōzō Temple

With an empty heart
I left society. How
deeply moved I am
when a snipe bursts from the field
in the autumn evening.

*

No one visits here
in my mountain hut
where I live alone.
But for this sweet loneliness,
it would be too bleak to bear.

*

This poor grass-roofed hut
of old brushwood may sound
miserable, but
I very quickly found it
altogether to my taste.

*

Tock, tock. The spring
water slowly drips down on
mossy rocks—but not
nearly enough for me
to draw for my hermitage.

*

This loneliness is
not simply the result
of autumn colors—
even mountain evergreens make
me feel like autumn evening.

*

He whose heart and soul
are at one with the great void
steps into the mist
and suddenly thinks himself
stepping right out of this world.

*

The skylark departs,
leaving in the wilderness
a small red lily.
Thus, without friend or attachment,
my heart remains alone.

*

Quite the contrary
to what I'd thought, passing clouds
are sometimes simply
the moon's entertainment,
its lovely decoration.

*

Deep in the mountains,
water splashes down the crags:
if I could stop it,
I'd go in search of wild nuts
that fall this time of year.

*

Along the trail's edge
beside a sparkling river
in the willow shade,
I lingered to take a nap—
lingered, and I'm still here.

*

Deep within the mountains,
the mind's moon brightly shines,
its light mirroring
all things everywhere, itself
mirrored in the enlightened mind.

*

Those who won't discard
all attachments to this world
and accept this life
are doomed to return like gold
to die again and again.

*

Even among those
who think themselves indifferent
toward most things,
it brings and inner shiver—
this first cool autumn wind.

*

Carried by breezes,
the blossoms all drift away.
I can't know where they go,
only that my heart remains
alone here deep within me.

*

I'd like to divide
myself in order to see,
among these mountains,
each and every flower
of every cherry tree.

*

Overseeing all
from high in the cherry tree,
even the flowers
grow sad—will they once again
return to greet the spring?

*

Touring Kisagata by Boat

In Kisagata,
the flowering cherry trees
vanish under waves—
until an old fisherman
rows out across blossoms.

*

By morning, the leaves
have fallen into silence,
the wind has finally parted,
like lovers after a night,
all talked out, now broken-hearted.

*

The titmouse perches
happily among its friends—
a reliable
roost safe among the branches
on the passania tree.

*

Deep in a ravine,
in a tree on the old farm,
a single dove sings out,
searching for a friend:
the lonely voice of evening.

*

Whom is it calling
in this high mountain village,
that lonely cuckoo?
When he came here, he came
alone, just wanting a life.

*

On the clear mirror,
just a single speck of dust.
And yet we see it
before all else, our poor world
having come to what it is.

*

In Tsu country,
that bright Naniwa spring—
was it only a dream?
Only withered reeds remain,
blanketed by cold winds.

*

Dead, I'll lie forever
alone beneath a blanket
of cold moss
remembering what is learned
only from dew and dark stone.

*

At the Grave of the Poet Fujiwara Sanekata
(d.998, Exiled from the Imperial Court in Kyoto)

He left us nothing
but his own eternal name—
just that final stroke.
On his poor grave on the moor,
one sees only pampas grass.

*

If possible,
I hope to be beneath
those last cherry blossoms
when I die—right around the time
of the full moon of spring.

*

The mind is all sky,
the heart utterly empty,
and the perfect moon
is completely transparent
entering western mountains.

All Here

for Ella Addison Wiegers, B. Nov., 1999

Body of dew, mind
of empty sky—the prelude
and the afterword

★

Under bare willows,
pond frogs sing about old age
while girls dream of princes

Part Three

R.I.P.

Lester Taylor's ranch
went tits up when the market
for range beef collapsed.
More than forty years have passed,
and The Mountain broken up—

all for grain-fed beef
suffering in standing lots
across the heartlands.
My father's farm went under
when he grew too old to work.

The American
Century passes, leaving
behind its corpses
and cadavers, its Lester
Taylors and Sam Burns Hamills,

its sad old Ghost Dance,
the demise of the Bar A
and thousands like it.
We have Cardiac Burgers
and cruelty to show for it,

fast food, the service
industry, and little thought
of what we order.
Poisoned by the Agribiz,
progress marches right along.

They were surrogate
fathers to me, those hard men
whose hearts must have been
carved out of granite to choose
such cold, solitary duties.

If they knew a name
for love, I never heard it.
Theirs was a beauty
known only within the bones,
learned from life with animals—

animals to tend,
animals birthing, dying,
refusing to eat
or getting stranded in snow
in a sudden big northern.

They loved that other
way of life—often enough
meaning poverty—
expressed in the unstated
convictions of all their days.

Love's an animal
that had no voice, a quick glance
at the right moment,
or perhaps just a hint of
a smile—almost unnoticed.

A good horse listens
to a rider's knees. I learned
soon enough to bite
my tongue or face a whipping.
What I demanded of them

they too demanded
from me: Not love, but respect.
I'll love them always.
But I was a fool then: I
imitated their folly.

Tommy Played the Blues

for Stephen Kuusisto

When I was in college, my blind friend
got all the girls. I used to chide him
for deflowering debutantes at whim.
There was always an angel on his arm

to lead the way through heaven's gates
into realms of utter ecstasy
he'd disclose in blissful detail, ice
in his tequila popping with delight.

"Sometimes I think they want me just
because I'm blind," he laughed, adding,
"and that's okay. I'm really not above
the pity lay. Truth is, I pity them."

He slowly sipped his drink and grinned,
"I teach them Braille." Do you fall in love
so easily, I asked. "No. Love fails me
because my music is my everything."

"One Who Studies the Past in Order to Learn the Present Is Fit to Teach."

for Emily Troutman, archivist
9th day, 11th month, 4698, Year of the Iron Dragon

K'ung-fu Tzu walked by the dynastic temple,
mourning the death of his friend, Yen Hui.
Perhaps he meditated on Lao Tzu's
"Beauty and ugliness have one origin,"

and asked himself whether virtue did not
likewise rise from a root. His old friend
had struggled to be a virtuous man.
There were dark clouds on the horizon.

A disciple, Tzu Kung, wanted to lift
his master's spirit, but K'ung-fu Tzu turned away.
"No one knows me," he said. "They call me,
'that dog from a house in mourning.'"

Tzu Kung asked, "How can you say such a thing?"
I thought of such things this morning,
a little frightened and embarrassed by
one who has looked into my history.

How will time judge me? Damned if I know.
My accomplishment is, I got up today.
I tried to write a poem. K'ung-fu Tzu said,
"The study of the low penetrates the high."

Winter Solstice, 1998

At twenty degrees,
dry logs split with a loud pop.
I burn inside a book.

*

Nothing quite so cold
as a winter night alone
talking with the dead.

"Praise a Fool and Make Him Useful"

Now that I've squandered
almost a lifetime going
to school on those old
dead poets who rabble-roused
or retreated into a

kind of solitude
few can understand—now that
I have invested
forty years in the struggle
not to struggle, following

the ancient teachings,
how astonishing it is,
how embarrassing,
to wake up some days and feel—
well—almost respectable.

Below Clay Hill

I did not come this far
only to die in Johnson, Vermont
but I could live here for a time
where the Gihon River flows under cold spring winds,

I could walk Clay Hill and see across the slope
to Marshall Walker's place and fall in love
again with the legends of those men
who lived here long ago, in harsher times.

Still, Venus in the west, twilit sky turquoise blue.
"Hereabouts yer 'creek' is called a brook."
True, I'm a stranger in this land, a visitor
who came because I know the man

and work that made this place, his writing shack,
a mansion of the art. Now shadows roll
over rolling wooded hills and the descent
beckons. The poet's house is made of words.

Unsolicited

So much ambition
and such futility in
everyone's poems.
It's galling and quite lovely
that we dare write them at all.

Sonnet on the Thirty-second Anniversary of My Internship as an Editor

Day after day after day, they arrive,
letters with hopes and dreams, egos and tears
staining every line. "I was abused
as a child and want to share my dysfunctions
with the world." "I am dying of cancer
and this is my story." "He ruined my
whole life, and now my poems expose him."
"I'm not really a poet, but would you
please publish my poems?" "Dear Editor:
You are obviously a piece of shit
who wouldn't know a poem if it pissed
in your pocket. Cordially, the poet."

And then there is the one poem, one line,
that makes it all somehow begin again.

On Being Asked About Retirement

For most white male Americans my age,
it would be nothing special, I suppose,
to drive an hour to a shopping mall
to buy a summer's clothes.

Year after year I bought a pair of jeans
and a couple of shirts from the discount rack
to mark the beginning of summer.
But suddenly I find myself being paid

for doing just what I've always done—
giving poetry away. Entering
the middle class at my age makes me,
I admit it, nervous. Nevertheless,

I like this Van Heusen, and that Arrow
is awfully nice. I've never owned
a necktie or a suit, and I don't suppose
I'm the least inclined to now.

Put me in a suit and I'd be fake
as a presidential smile. Same old jeans
to greet my day. For an editor,
the crap factor's deep some days.

I'll buy myself some teeth
and a sexy dress for my beautiful wife
and celebrate with *sake* and *unagi,*
and that's a change of life.

It sounds a little odd
to say it this way, but I'm employed
in the service of poetry. I got a job.
And job security.

Rising

December 24, 1998

No romance here, but a willingness to age
and die at the speed of sound. —Jim Harrison

It's time again not to push a metaphor too far,
but when solstice falls on frozen ground
and snow falls steadily on the water, islands
dissolving in the chalky distance,
and only a single crow in the sky,
I think of Yesenin at the doctor's,
finding the old woman whose legs were blue,
Akhmatova so solemn at the gates,
Tu Fu huddled over his charcoal stove,
trying to thaw his fingers enough
to hold his writing brush. Bashō listened
in the silence to ice crack his rice jar.
The sky is slate white—a chalkboard
erased ten thousand times.

Winter solstice. Nothing inherently holy
in that, except the days grow longer now,
the cold a little less cold because it comes
on the wings of spring. It's Ramadan, Chanukah,
Kwanzaa and Christmas, and for a moment,
the missiles have been silenced. The world
is strangely still, trees black against the sky.
Hayden's alone in his little house in the eastern cold
as I am alone in mine, a continent away.
He writes of dialing 911:
"A helicopter ride would be fun."

Li Po looked up at a pale, thin moon
and raised his sake cup. Not much has changed.

Those who claim to know murder those
they call false prophets while science
improves their tools. There is death
in Jerusalem, frozen death among the homeless
all across the heartland. A president
is impeached, and the stock market rises.
Tibet is Chinese and the Makah want whales.

I got up from my *zafu* in the first gray light
and blew out the candle and went into the kitchen
and turned on the lights; I made a latte
and went outside and stood
shivering on the deck in the last of the dark,
remembering ten thousand dawns I watched
emerge from trees and mountains.

I remembered my wife rushing in from the garden,
"Let's go make love—the dragonflies are fucking!"
What man was I when I cleared this land
and built my hermitage? What man today?
I remembered the dogs I buried.
Slowly, a few snowy trees turned from dark to white.
This world is frost on an old man's breath,
memory rushing into memory.

Twenty years ago, on a warm midsummer night,
Gary Snyder got up on stage at the Town Tavern,
beer mug in hand, and recited "Ode to the West Wind"
in his indelibly lovely voice
to a boisterous, cheering crowd. It made me
feel alive at the speed of sound. Outside,
the same moon rose above the water
that Wang Wei watched rise over the river
a thousand years before. It was the same night.
It was the same poem.

To Bill and Kris

I never wanted
a cell phone or electronic
mail, a Cadillac
or a limousine to cruise
the Information Highway.

A dusty back road
through obdurate relics of
civilization
is where I've built my retreat.
Give me a California

Job Drawer, a press
I can ink by hand, cotton
fiber paper made
by hand in France, Italy
or Japan, and let me be.

I like the feel of
the poem as it takes shape
in my hands, the smell
of damp paper, oil, type wash,
the hum and clunk of the press.

Technology is,
of itself, neither good nor
evil, but bequeaths
and reveals what's in the heart
already: whether pine breeze

or voracious
appetite. It's not that I
reject the comforts
of modern technology—
I want my running water,

electricity,
a warm house in deep winter.
More is not better—
not always. The marketplace
attracts a gaggle of thieves.

Rats seek the rice bowl.
I've spent a lifetime getting
a little out of
line, content with solitude,
half a recluse, a throwback,

building with my hands
this little Buddhist retreat
we named Kage-an,
Shadow Hermitage, under
the dark cedars of the North-

west coast. This is not
a retreat from the world's ways,
as some Buddhists think,
but an entryway, a door
opening on the real world.

I keep things simple
in my hands and heart. I was,
from the start, a fool—
stubborn, happy in my work,
making a gift no one wants

and giving it all
away. I still remember
the first time I heard
a single alder leaf fall
through autumn trees, a click, click

as it tumbled down.
You can't give away that sound.
You can hold the moon
between your hands, but you can't
hold it long. The simple fact

of poetry is
astonishment enough. That
and life's ironies
duly noted as I write
this epistle on my Mac.

Seattle Spring

After ninety-four
consecutive days of rain,
even frogs don't sing.

Part Four

On Being Invited to Write a Poem
on the Theme of Shelter

No shelter, nowhere
to seek refuge—only this
falling mist of June

*

shelter: from the Old English
scild, meaning *shield*, and *scell* or *scyll*,
meaning *shell*.

But who can live within a shell
or under a shield—that would
shield us from *what*?

The ancient poet sang,
With sky for a blanket
and earth for a pillow,

which, depending upon context,
may be an awful curse,

but which he found to be a blessing.
I have sheltered battered women
and battered children, and, homeless,
sought shelter myself

from various storms. Worse,
I have heard and ignored the voice that warned,
Be careful what you ask for.

I learned late
and alone
that what I sought was not a shield,
a shell, a shelter,

but what I alone could make—
so make myself at home.

Assay

The sum of this year's
harvest after all the deer—
one perfect red plum

Epithalamion for Laura and Michael

After all these years,
the same sun burning through mist,
the slosh, slosh of tides.
Deer gorge on fallen apples.
Everything we need: right here.

New Math

Epithalamion for Nina and John

When two become one,
that one is greater than two—
how could anyone
otherwise surrender such
indecorous quantities

of greed as are in-
vested in the pronoun *I*,
subordinating
self for that which is plural?
Ryōkan points at this bright moon

and knows his finger
and the moon and this long night
make one. The marriage
is born of nuptials, plural,
the exchange of mutual vows

born in the Latin
nuptiae—also plural—
many vows making
one ceremony—wedding—
making the one of many.

This from *nubere*,
the taking of a husband.
And *husband*? —from the
old Norse *husbondi*, the house-
dweller, the conservator.

And wife is a *wyf*,
a veiled one, embodiment
of the mystery
that makes of the plural one,
her secrets revealed only

to the husbandman
with whom she builds the temple
that is a garden
witnessed in the *Song of Songs*
through centuries of devotion.

We become the sum
of all we give away.
The garden and the
gardeners, the soil and sun,
love and labor: all make one.

Upon Receipt of a Gift of Chopsticks

Those who speak don't know.
Those who know know beyond words.
The gift's a kōan
to be carried on one's way
and savored, even cherished.

Silver-tipped *hashi*
and a slender knife encased
in a silver-tipped
scabbard, wood worn with ages
of human care—if I ate

with splendid *hashi*
such as these, ghosts of shoguns
would sit beside me;
how-many-hundreds-of-years
would fill my mouth with each bite?

I'll lightly polish
the silver just once, to clean
those few old stains. Then
I'll hang it close beside my
butsudan—there where I bow.

It's easy to mis-
understand the true nature
of the gift, which is only
an emblem for the unnamed,
unnamable mystery.

Cookin' with Jane

Shoyu, olive oil
and a pinch of wasabe
for searing salmon
before carefully slicing
warm, delicious sashimi—

Jane's old fruit label
promises "buxom melons,"
our watermelon
just watermelon, no breasts
suggested, in the freezer.

While Tammy Wynette
sings of standing by her man,
Jane breaks up lettuce
and slices ripe tomatoes
and explains the barbecue

where we'll soon enough
smell fresh ahi on the grill.
Shiitake and
Portobello mushrooms sliced
thick and sautéed in butter.

We've found a bottle
of Momokawa sake—
all we could ask for,
and maybe a little more,
as when a good friend arrives.

What does it mean, Jane,
that these joys are my greatest,
the sacramental
moment finally realized
together after all these

many, many years?
The ocotillo blossoms
only after rain.
After that harsh Tucson sun,
the evening is a breeze.

In making a toast
the Japanese say, *Kanpai!*—
in Chinese, *Gum-bai*—
meaning bottoms up, the cup
turned to lifted chin which then

lowers to suggest
a little bow to honor
the honorable
drinking companion or guest.
And thus this salutation:

the old tradition,
from Sappho and all those Greeks
to Master Tu Fu,
Chuang Tzu and the old Chinese,
poor poets drink, praise, and feast.

Great American Nude

She yawns and draws her stocking up.
I study her right breast
in perfect profile,
armpit to elbow framing the shot,
thinking how I might paint this view
with a broad palette knife,
slopping globs
of heavy red and brown
over a two-foot nipple
on an eight-foot canvas,
paint too thick to run,

but sagging,
as our own flesh comes to sag
on the bone with age. You're
staring, she says,
folding her arms across her chest
for just a moment, a smile
at the corners of her mouth,

and I look down
at my own heavy breasts,
thatch of white hair between,
and look up at her again,
feeling like
an unflattering portrait by Chuck Close,
perspective up the nose.

She is so beautiful slipping on her blouse
that I think perhaps
that too must go into the painting,
soft white cotton barely rising
in a corner of the frame,

and I add blue and purple with my fingers—
just enough to suggest the veins—
feeling that old familiar curve enlarged
a dozen times, colors intensified
as through a lens,

splotches of orange and yellow,
white and pale pink, oh great
American nude without torso or head,
without limb,
the great breast like a mountain—
grand teton—

reminding me of the light that breaks
through steep multicolored canyons
in the autumn dawn
and of the men
who were our fathers
searching that great unknown.

But just then she sighs
heavily and says,
Why this long silence? She says,
I got to run.
And I am struck dumb
with fear of losing the image I was concentrating on,

and as she pauses to kiss my cheek
and touch my lower lip
with just a fingertip,
she looks into my eyes and says,
You know,
I've spent my whole damned life
loving lonely men.

Road Hog Sutra

Bodhidharma's face—
big bushy brow and long beard
and dangling earring—
on my lapel pin prompts a
postal worker to ask, "Hey!

Who's that biker you got there?"

Bobbitt, the Trial

Lorena Bobbitt took a knife
and gave poor John a wicked slice,
then took his penis for a ride
and threw it out the window.

When at last
it was reattached,
John said he hoped that it would grow
and serve him even better.

He, found innocent of abuse—
or rape, in any case—refused
to ask for vengeance from the court.
He said she lied about the bruises.

Now she's proclaimed, by some,
a hero. On the morality scale,
zero sum: no honor,
and no excuses.

Bobbitt

John Wayne Bobbitt, I salute you who high-
fived the doctor when your penis was found
and brought in to be sewn back on. It's true,
little things do, after all, mean a lot.
From tiny acorns stately oaks do grow.

"In sex, he never thinks of me," your wife,
in cuffs, confessed, "and so I cut it off."
And there followed a slough of cruel jokes,
charges—you were treated like a woman.
Consider yourself fortunate in this:

although you've yet to sample wedded bliss,
you may live to try again, so I've heard,
and thereby shall be doubly fortunate
if your name should fade from our lexicon—
you almost lived to end up as a verb.

Seducing the Sparrow

Birds live in a world without karma.
—Morris Graves

Why must the noble rose
bristle before it blooms, and why
must the frost declare
allegiance to the dew?

Don't tell me the robin's
forlorn invitation
could not be denied.
I've heard the magpie's lies.

Outside my window,
twenty-seven juncos
consort in a cedar tree,
fat and happy to be free

of all desire—ah, but
that's not true! See
how they dance and turn
when I throw out the seed.

Arachnophobia

Because he was terrified by spiders,
he blamed them
for anything that went wrong.
At night
when he went to bed, he would look up
and see a tiny web and get up
and knock it down with a broom.
And then he would dream
that he was almost dead,
and that spiders were weaving him
into a silky thick sarcophagus,
and he would wake up screaming, clawing at the air.

The spiders didn't seem to mind.
They spun their webs in cracks and crevices
high in the rafters, and slunk back into shadows
to weave their savage dreams.

Even after he moved from the country house
into the new airtight condominium
sprayed with insecticides and sealed tight,
he continued to dream of glittering spider-eyes
watching as he slept,
patient, in their webs—
vampire spiders,
spiders of darkness and of light,
stitching his lips shut tight
until he couldn't even scream.
Night after night, he woke in a sweat.

He turned to a therapist for help.
The therapist told him spiders represent
an archetype, the devouring

mother of his psyche,
and that he needed treatment.

The therapist asked him how he felt
about his penis, and told him
he was trying to return to the safety of the womb
but was frightened by the image of enclosing darkness,
or perhaps he felt his mother
was consuming him
and that was why he dreamed of spiders
wrapping him at night.

The therapist told him he needed to learn
to understand his own sexuality,
and clarify turbulent feelings
about his mother. The therapist
explained how we demonize
whatever we do not understand.
The therapist promised to help.

With help from his therapist,
he eventually overcame his dread
and developed a prodigious sexual appetite
that left him too exhausted to dream.
He lived a long life and helped many others
overcome a variety of phobias, until,
in the end, he was devoured
by the spiders of delight.

Plain Dumb Luck

Forty-two years ago, in the cold
pitch black of the hours before dawn,
I huddled in a cell in Fredonia, Arizona,
rolling cigarettes from a Bull Durham pouch,
locked up for the crime of being
fourteen and homeless. How many nights
did I watch the stars through that barred skylight?
I no longer remember. With no one
to sign me out, there I sat,
watching as stars, one after the next,
blinked and burned out and the sky
grew inky black until it erased the bars
above my head. I smoked and sulked.

Dawn burned away the clouds and I ate
shit-on-a-shingle and the old sheriff
finally came and let me out, telling me,
"Go back home, son," as if
I had any choice at all. Home was the road
for a kid whose other home was hell.
I'd rather steal than taste that belt again.
I stole. But none of that matters now.

Here in the January dark, dawn
two hours below the horizon,
forty-two years down the pike,
I remember that night as clearly as if
it were only yesterday. The condemned know why.
There were other nights in other cells
during those troublesome years. What I had
was poetry and blues. Miles played
So What and Kind of Blue. Coltrane,
Dexter, and Rexroth got me through. I still

have my old Signet *On the Road*, tatters
and yellowed, but I don't read it any more.

The old man died long ago. And the woman
who darkened my days for forty-five years?
Dust. Dust on my boots, a dusty book
all but forgotten on the shelf. Everyone
knows that story well. But when the man
on NPR mentions Fredonia, Arizona,
I suddenly realize where I am—
My wife sleeps peacefully in the home
I built of poverty, poetry, and love. Turning
off the radio, I sit alone, counting breaths
in the dark until counting disappears,
bowing to the dark itself, surprised to be
the luckiest son-of-a-bitch alive.

The Orchid Flower

Just as I wonder
whether it's going to die,
the orchid blossoms

and I can't explain why it
moves my heart, why such pleasure

comes from one small bud
on a long spindly stem, one
blood red gold flower

opening at mid-summer,
tiny, perfect in its hour.

Even to a white-
haired craggy poet, it's
purely erotic,

pistil and stamen, pollen,
dew of the world, a spoonful

of earth, and water.
Erotic because there's death
at the heart of birth,

drama in those old sunrise
prisms in wet cedar boughs,

deepest mystery
in washing evening dishes
or teasing my wife,

who grows, yes, more beautiful
because one of us will die.

A Woodsplitter's Meditation

I.
Early October mist pours through the trees
surrounding Kage-an, bringing autumn
chills that send me out to the woodpile with
my new splitting maul. I test it simply,
popping dry alder I cut two years ago.

Two stellar jays come to see, yammering
loudly from the low boughs of a cedar tree
grown tall from a nurse log. I split hemlock,
spruce and fir I bucked last winter. Each pops
open like a book, pages glued with sap.

I have read this book, and so have the jays.
It is written in ordinary days
and deeds addressing all temporal desire.
I laugh too, then go in and light the fire.

II.
I began this poem a month ago,
then put it in a drawer. Since then I've been
to California and seen Hood Canal
canopied with orange and yellow maple.
Autumn chill turned to early winter cold.

My bones grow stiffer as I grow older,
but I do as well as I am able.
I heard my friend's husband died suddenly,
leaving me, bad habits and all, mourning,
and, being his elder, feeling guilty.

Time is beauty, I think sometimes. I love
these last brown leaves as I love growing old,
sowing last month's plantings, tending this day's
business at the woodpile, facing the snow.

III.
I have no wisdom to ease her mourning.
I have no wisdom at all. I carry
the wood I split and build fires in the night,
and huddle in my skin. What do I know?
Leaves fall, trees grow. The snow is magical.

Time is beauty. Time together, time apart.
The woodsplitter's meditation contains
no answers, only questions, and seeks the heart
of what time makes us: rings and scars, bruisings
and vows and destinies never imagined.

What can I know of anyone's loss? I
invest in the certainty of my death,
no time to squander and no need to rush,
but when she asks, Where shall I turn? I'm hushed.

IV.
Shall I say Li Ch'ing-chao mourned beautifully?
That Yuan Chen's great elegies are great
because he speaks so simply? I'm silent
because my ignorance overwhelms me—
I bow to what I cannot understand.

The Upaya teaches "skillful means," the
Kannon long life sutra means compassion,
the loud cracks of my splitting maul recite
a hundred temple bells, a hundred sutras.
For whom? For what, without a little heat?

I will tell her I have not learned to grieve
as a widow grieves, and what will it mean?
The wood crib full, the fire lit, I sit
alone in dying light and slowly breathe.

Notes on the Poems

"Chuang Tzu and the First Noble Truth" is for J. P. Seaton, with whom I translated *The Essential Chuang Tzu* (Shambhala Publications).

"Poem in the Margins of the *Shōyō Roku*" —The *Shōyō Roku* is a collection of one hundred Zen "cases" or kōans, called *The Book of Serenity* in Thomas Cleary's translation, and is to Soto Zen what *The Blue Cliff Record* is to Rinzai Zen.

"*Zuihitsu*" was inspired in part by the poetry of Kimiko Hahn. The haiku by Issa reads, "As old age arrives, / considering just the day's length / can move one to tears."

"Fifteen Stitches" is for my friend Wayne Larrabee, a Seattle plastic surgeon who, for many years, has repaired the broken faces and bodies of severely-battered women.

"Sisyphus" was inspired by some correspondence with Hayden Carruth and Jim Harrison and steals a line or two from each. Referenced poems also include the great modern Greek poet George Seferis, and the story of the fisherman can be found in *The Essential Chuang Tzu*.

"Lives of a Poet: Saigyō's Solitude"—Saigyō Hōshō (1118–1190) took Buddhist vows and became a renowned mountain hermit and a predominant figure in Japan's long tradition of Buddhist nature poetry, a model and inspiration for Bashō, Issa, Ryōkan and many others. These translations are dedicated to my friend and co-worker, Michael Wiegers, whose good faith and support allow me to deepen my own solitude when necessary.

"Tommy Played the Blues" was inspired by Stephen Kuusisto, author of *Planet of the Blind* and *Only Bread, Only Light*.

"One Who Studies the Past in Order to Learn the Present is Fit to Teach" —The title is from Confucius (K'ung-fu Tzu) and the dedication an echo of classical Chinese "headers" which frame many court poems.

"Praise a Fool and Make Him Useful" —Another title from K'ung-fu Tzu.

"Below Clay Hill" refers to Hayden Carruth. My thanks to the Vermont Studio Center for hosting my visit to my old friend's legendary "cow shed" where he composed so many masterful poems.

"A Woodsplitter's Meditation" is for Carol Muske-Dukes, following the untimely death of her husband, the actor David Dukes. The elegies of Yuan Chen and Li Ch'ing-chao are among the most revered in all of Chinese poetry.

Acknowledgments

Bloomsbury Review: "'Praise a Fool and Make Him Useful'";

Blue Beat Jacket (Japan): "In Memoriam: Morris Graves";

Faultline: "'One Who Studies the Past in Order to Learn the Present Is Fit to Teach'";

Five Points: "New Math," "Great American Nude," "Plain Dumb Luck" "New Math";

Lyric: "Below Clay Hill";

The Nation: "Seducing the Sparrow," "The Orchid Blossom";

Richard Hugo House: "On Being Invited to Write a Poem on the Theme of Shelter";

Great River Review: "Sisyphus," "Zuihitsu";

Prairie Schooner: "A Woodsplitter's Meditation";

Prosodia: "Chuang Tzu and the First Noble Truth," "Rising";

Two Rivers: "Poem in the Margins of the *Shōyō Roku*."

Several of the translations gathered in "Saigyō's Solitude" were originally published in *The Virginia Quarterly Review;* others were originally published in *Only Companion: Japanese Poems of Love & Longing* (Shambhala Publications, 1997); an elegant limited edition of these poems was published as *Saigyō Hōshō: A Troubled Heart & Other Waka* by Tricia Treacy at Pointed Press.

About the Author

Editor, translator and poet, Sam Hamill is the author of a dozen books of original poetry, including *Destination Zero: Poems 1970-1995* and *Gratitude* (BOA, 1998) as well as three collections of essays. He has also translated more than two dozen volumes of poetry from ancient Greek, Latin, Estonian, Japanese and Chinese. These translations include *Crossing the Yellow River: Three Hundred Poems from the Chinese* (BOA 2000); *Narrow Road to the Interior & Other Writings of Bashō; The Spring of My Life & Selected Haiku by Kobayashi Issa; River of Stars: Selected Poems of Yosano Akiko* (with Keiko Matsui Gibson). He has been the recipient of fellowships from the National Endowment for the Arts, the Guggenheim Foundation, the Lila Wallace-Readers Digest Fund, the Andrew Mellon Fund and has received two Washington Governor's Arts Awards. He is director of the Port Townsend Writers' Conference and Founding Editor of Copper Canyon Press.

BOA EDITIONS, LTD.

AMERICAN POETS CONTINUUM SERIES

No. 1   *The Fuhrer Bunker: A Cycle*
of Poems in Progress
W. D. Snodgrass

No. 2   *She*
M. L. Rosenthal

No. 3   *Living With Distance*
Ralph J. Mills, Jr.

No. 4   *Not Just Any Death*
Michael Waters

No. 5   *That Was Then: New and*
Selected Poems
Isabella Gardner

No. 6   *Things That Happen Where*
There Aren't Any People
William Stafford

No. 7   *The Bridge of Change:*
Poems 1974–1980
John Logan

No. 8   *Signatures*
Joseph Stroud

No. 9   *People Live Here: Selected*
Poems 1949–1983
Louis Simpson

No. 10   *Yin*
Carolyn Kizer

No. 11   *Duhamel: Ideas of Order in*
Little Canada
Bill Tremblay

No. 12   *Seeing It Was So*
Anthony Piccione

No. 13   *Hyam Plutzik: The Collected*
Poems

No. 14   *Good Woman: Poems and a*
Memoir 1969–1980
Lucille Clifton

No. 15   *Next: New Poems*
Lucille Clifton

No. 16   *Roxa: Voices of the Culver*
Family
William B. Patrick

No. 17   *John Logan: The Collected Poems*

No. 18   *Isabella Gardner: The*
Collected Poems

No. 19   *The Sunken Lightship*
Peter Makuck

No. 20   *The City in Which I Love You*
Li-Young Lee

No. 21   *Quilting: Poems 1987–1990*
Lucille Clifton

No. 22   *John Logan: The Collected*
Fiction

No. 23   *Shenandoah and Other Verse*
Plays
Delmore Schwartz

No. 24   *Nobody Lives on Arthur*
Godfrey Boulevard
Gerald Costanzo

No. 25   *The Book of Names: New and*
Selected Poems
Barton Sutter

No. 26   *Each in His Season*
W. D. Snodgrass

No. 27   *Wordworks: Poems Selected*
and New
Richard Kostelanetz

No. 28   *What We Carry*
Dorianne Laux

No. 29   *Red Suitcase*
Naomi Shihab Nye

No. 30   *Song*
Brigit Pegeen Kelly

No. 31   *The Fuehrer Bunker:*
The Complete Cycle
W. D. Snodgrass

No. 32   *For the Kingdom*
Anthony Piccione

No. 33   *The Quicken Tree*
Bill Knott

No. 34   *These Upraised Hands*
William B. Patrick

No. 35   *Crazy Horse in Stillness*
William Heyen

Colophon

Dumb Luck, Poems by Sam Hamill,
was set with Monotype Dante & Rococo ornaments
by Richard Foerster, York Beach, Maine.
The cover was designed by Lisa Mauro/Mauro Design.
Manufacturing was by McNaughton & Gunn,
Saline, Michigan.

✦

Publication of this book was made possible, in part,
by the special support of the following people:
Carol & Ron Bailey • Laure-Anne Bosselaar & Kurt Brown
Nancy & Alan Cameros
Ron & Susan Dow • Dr. Henry & Beverly French
Dane & Judy Gordon • Suzanne & Gerard Gouvernet
Marge & Don Grinols • Kip & Deb Hale • William Hauser
Grant & Siobhan Holcomb • Peter & Robin Hursh
Robert & Willy Hursh • Dorothy & Henry Hwang
Donald & Linda Kaplan • Archie & Pat Kutz
Boo Poulin • Deborah Ronnen • David Ryon
Jane Schuster • Robert B. Shea
Liesl Slabaugh & Joseph Bednarik • Allen & Suzy Spencer
Sue S. Stewart & Stephen L. Raymond
Katherine S. Taylor • Robert & Lee Ward
Pat & Michael Wilder • Mark Williams • Sabra & Clifton Wood

✦